The

TREASURE PRINCIPLE
WORKSHOP

Student Workbook

CROWN FINANCIAL MINISTRIES
True Financial Freedom

CROWN.ORG

ISBN 10: 1-56427-157-9
ISBN 13: 978-1-56427-157-0

This workshop is based on content from *The Treasure Principle* by Randy Alcorn (ISBN 1-57673-780-2) and is created in partnership with Generous Giving, www.GenerousGiving.org.

Scripture quotations are taken from the Holy Bible: New International Version, copyright 1973, 1978, 1984 by the International Bible Society. Used by permission of Zondervan Bible Publishers.

December 2007 Edition

Contents

THANK YOU FOR YOUR INTEREST IN LEARNING GOD'S WAY OF HANDLING money. You may be surprised to learn that the Lord said a lot about finances. There are more than 2,350 verses in the Bible that deal with money and possessions.

The Treasure Principle Workshop is one of a series of Crown Financial Ministries' "Workshops in a Box." Each workshop uses biblical principles to address a practical topic, such as getting out of debt, investing, budgeting, what engaged couples need to know about money, and many others.

The Treasure Principle Workshop contains 6 sessions, each addressing a different area of giving and lasting about 25 minutes. This video may be used in a Sunday school class, weekend seminar, small group, or in other settings.

The Student Workbook helps participants apply the principles they are learning and should be used by each person. The "Video Notes" section is an outline containing blank spaces for the participants to fill in key words as they watch the video.

The "Discussion Questions" section provides several questions to discuss with the group after each video. Before you end each class, you may want to take prayer requests and record these in the back of the Student Workbook.

For those who wish to better grasp and apply the principles, the Student Workbook contains an optional "Dig Deeper and Learn More" section. It includes a Scripture to memorize, selected verses to look up, and questions to answer.

Finally, the "Audio Testimonies" section in Chapters 2-5 contains powerful and encouraging testimonies from individuals who have found the secret of the treasure principle. It is provided by our partner in ministry, Generous Giving, as optional support to the principles learned in each chapter of the study. Their stories will inspire you and your small group to search and find the treasure principle, too!

During this video series we will occasionally refer to the Crown Financial Ministries church program. We hope you'll decide to enroll in Crown's small group study and learn more about Crown's other outstanding materials and studies.

For those who wish to learn more about giving, the most effective ministry is Generous Giving. It seeks to motivate followers of Jesus Christ toward greater biblical generosity.

Please visit their Web site at www.GenerousGiving.org. You will find an outstanding selection of books, tapes, and many other tools designed to help you go deeper in your giving journey.

CHAPTER ONE

BURIED TREASURE

*"He is no fool who gives what he
cannot keep to gain what he
cannot lose."*
—Jim Elliot

M ANY PEOPLE ARE EXPERIENCING FINANCIAL CHALLENGES. They are facing growing debt, little or no savings, inadequate income, and no plans for their financial future. Surveys reveal that more than half of all divorces are a result of financial tension in the home.

Others are financially sound, but suffocating materialism has robbed them of their spiritual vitality. They are not spending their resources in eternally significant ways.

Fortunately, the Bible has the answers to these financial difficulties—it contains more than 2,350 verses dealing with money and possessions. More of these verses deal with the area of giving than any other financial subject.

The Treasure Principle Workshop, based on Randy Alcorn's best-selling book, *The Treasure Principle*, will help you gain God's perspective on giving. The Lord intends giving to be one of the most blessed and joyful experiences of our Christian life.

 **VIDEO NOTES**

1. The story is captured by Jesus in a single verse: *"The kingdom of heaven is like _____ hidden in a field. When a man found it, he hid it again, and then in his _____ went and sold all he had and bought that field"* (Matthew 13:44).

THE MONEY CONNECTION

2. The parable of hidden treasure is one of many references Jesus made to money and possessions. In fact, _____ % of everything Christ said relates to this topic.

3. Why did Jesus put such an emphasis on money and possessions? Because there's a fundamental connection between our _____ lives and how we think about and handle _____.

4. We may try to divorce our faith and our finances, but God sees them as _____.

5. John the Baptist couldn't talk about spirituality without talking about how to handle _____ and possessions.

6. The traveler made short-term sacrifices to obtain a long-term _____.

7. Christ's story about treasure in the field is an object lesson concerning _____ treasure.

8. No matter how great the value of that earthly fortune, it would be _____ in eternity.

9. *"Do not store up for yourselves treasures on earth, where moth and rust destroy, and where thieves break in and steal. But store up for yourselves treasures in heaven, where moth and rust do not destroy, and where thieves*

do not break in and steal. *For where your treasure is, there your*
_____ *will be also"* (Matthew 6:19-21).

10. Consider what Jesus is saying: "Do not store up for yourselves treasures on earth." Why not? Because earthly treasures are bad? No. Because they won't _____.

11. When Jesus warns us not to store up treasures on earth, it's not just because wealth might be lost; it's because wealth will _____ be lost.

A TREASURE MENTALITY

12. Jesus doesn't just tell us where not to put our treasures. He also gives the best _____ advice you'll ever hear: *"Store up for yourselves _____ in heaven"* (Matthew 6:20).

13. "Store up *for yourselves*." Doesn't it seem strange that Jesus _____ us to do what's in our own best interests?

THE TREASURE PRINCIPLE

14. The Treasure Principle: "You can't _____ it with you—but you can _____ it on ahead."

15. Anything that we put into God's hands will be ours for _____.

16. If we give instead of keep, if we invest in the eternal instead of the _____, we store up treasures in heaven that will never stop paying dividends.

17. Christ, the ultimate investment counselor, takes it further. He says, "Don't ask how your investment will be paying off in just thirty years. Ask how it will be paying off in thirty _____ years."

CHAPTER SUMMARY BY RANDY ALCORN

1. Faith and finances are inseparable.
2. Giving is the smart thing to do.
3. Develop a treasure mentality.
4. You can't take it with you, but you can send it on ahead.

 # DISCUSSION QUESTIONS

1. What surprised you in the video segment you just saw?

2. Describe your own experience in giving. What has been frustrating and what has been a blessing in your giving?

3. After viewing this first lesson of *The Treasure Principle Workshop*, describe the most important principle you learned.

4. How will applying this principle impact you?

DIG DEEPER AND LEARN MORE

Each session contains optional exercises you may do on your own that will help you learn and apply the Treasure Principle. They include a Scripture to memorize and some questions to answer.

SCRIPTURE TO MEMORIZE
"But store up for yourselves treasures in heaven, where moth and rust do not destroy, and where thieves do not break in and steal" (Matthew 6:20).

QUESTIONS TO ANSWER

1. Read *Luke 12:16-20*. List at least two principles it teaches.

2. Now read *Luke 12:21*. What important principle does it teach? What should it look like in your life?

3. Read *Mark 12:43-44*. What does this passage say to you? How will you apply it?

CHAPTER 2

COMPOUNDING JOY

*"The less I spent on myself and the more
I gave to others, the fuller of happiness
and blessing did my soul become."*
—Hudson Taylor

 VIDEO NOTES

1. *"Everything under heaven _____ to me"* (Job 41:11).

2. *"The earth is the Lord's, and _____ in it, the world, and all
   who live in it"* (Psalm 24:1).

Treasure Principle Key #1: God owns _____. I'm His
money manager.

3. The _____ carries no sense of entitlement to the assets he
   manages.

JOYFUL GIVING

4. We should be thinking like stewards, investment _____,
   always looking for the best place to invest the _____ money.

5. *"For we will all stand before God's judgment seat…. So then, each of us will give an* _____ *of himself to God"* (Romans 14:10, 12).

6. One of our central spiritual decisions is determining what is a reasonable amount to _____ _____. God expects us to set our own salaries.

7. Do you want more excitement in your life? Then start _____. *"God loves a* _____ *giver"* (2 Corinthians 9:7).

8. The cheerfulness often comes during and _____ the act of obedience, not before it.

Thunder, Lightning, and Grace

9. *"Out of the most severe trial, their overflowing joy and their extreme* _____ *welled up in rich* _____*"* (2 Corinthians 8:2).

10. Giving isn't a _____ of the rich. It's a privilege of the _____.

11. *"They urgently* _____ *with us for the privilege of sharing in this service to the saints"* (2 Corinthians 8:4).

12. *"We want you to know about the* _____ *that God has given the Macedonian churches"* (2 Corinthians 8:1).

13. As thunder follows lightning, giving follows _____.

14. And as the Macedonians knew, giving is simply the overflow of _____.

The Fringe Benefits of Giving

15. God said, *"I give to the Levites as their inheritance the tithes that the Israelites present as an offering to the* _____*"* (Numbers 18:24).

16. Before anything else, giving is an act of _____.

17. God says, *"If a man shuts his ears to the cry of the _____, he too will cry out and _____ be answered"* (Proverbs 21:13).

18. Another benefit of giving is _____.

19. _____ infuses life with joy. It interjects an _____ dimension into even the most ordinary day.

CHAPTER SUMMARY BY RANDY ALCORN

1. God owns everything. I'm His money manager.
2. Be a joyful giver.
3. It's a privilege to give.
4. Giving provides fringe benefits.

 **DISCUSSION QUESTIONS**

1. What are some benefits of recognizing that we are stewards rather than owners?

2. Thinking as an investment manager, what are some of the best places Scripture says to invest the Owner's money? Why?

3. How is our giving a response to the grace of God in our lives?

4. How is giving an act of worship?

5. Describe some of the fringe benefits of giving.

6. How does the following statement change your perspective on giving, "Giving isn't a luxury of the rich. It's a privilege of the poor"?

DIG DEEPER AND LEARN MORE

QUESTIONS TO ANSWER

1. Read *Psalm 50:10-11*; *Haggai 2:8*; *Leviticus 25:23*; and *Psalm 24:1*. What do these verses say about God's ownership? Do you consistently recognize this?

2. Read *Luke 16:10-13* and *1 Corinthians 4:2*. List at least four principles God has revealed for us as we manage His assets.

COMPOUNDING JOY

3. Read *2 Corinthians 8:1-5*. List at least four characteristics of the giving by the Macedonian churches.

4. Read *Isaiah 58:5-12* and *Matthew 25:31-46*. How would you describe God's concern for the poor and needy? How would you describe His plan for meeting their needs? Who do you think is the greatest beneficiary when we give to the poor?

5. How does this chapter affect your desire and plan for giving?

AUDIO TESTIMONY – SCOTT AND AMY

This section provides additional study and encouragement from individuals who have learned the secret of the Treasure Principle. After listening to the testimony on the CD in the back of this workbook, answer the questions below.

1. Scott and Amy talk about the role that fear played in causing them to live a frugal lifestyle while preventing them from giving sacrificially to God's work.

   I'm living frugally because I'm afraid of the future. I'm motivated by fear. I don't know how I'm going to provide the lifestyle I want to provide Amy. I don't know how I'm going to buy a home. I don't know how I'm going to provide for a college education for my kids. I don't know how I'm going to do the things I want to do. So the 90% we were saving off her income was in response to the fear that was motivating me.

   God calls us to be faithful managers of all our resources. How has fear impacted the balance between spending, saving and giving in your life? Do you live with a scarcity or abundance mentality regarding your financial resources?

2. God directed Scott and Amy to give generously from Amy's income in order to overcome their fear. Their obedience then caused them to experience a new freedom.

God was leading me as a response to this fear to give more aggressively from Amy's income. It was to look that fear in the face and do something aggressive to respond to it by giving money that I was planning and needing to face that fear with. I think about what it means to be a Christian and to live my life on the edge but rarely do I think about how that applies to my money and my finances. To be challenged in that area was a first for me. And it wasn't that it was a scary thing…but it felt very freeing. As we began to give, one of the immediate benefits was that the fear began to fall off.

How should God's promise to care for His children in Matthew 6:28-33 impact your saving versus giving decisions? How does culture's focus on your right to a comfortable retirement and lifestyle counter God's Word? Why do you think that their fear began to fall off when they began giving versus saving?

CHAPTER 3

EYES ON ETERNITY

"For the Son of Man is going to come in his Father's glory with his angels, and then he will reward each person according to what he has done" (Matthew 16:27).

VIDEO NOTES

ETERNAL REWARDS

1. God also grants us rewards for generous giving: *"Go, sell your possessions and give to the poor, and you will have treasure in _____"* (Matthew 19:21).

2. Jesus is keeping track of our smallest acts of kindness: *"If anyone gives even a cup of cold water to one of these little ones because he is my disciple, I tell you the truth, he will certainly not lose his _____"* (Matthew 10:42).

3. Jesus said, *"If you have not been trustworthy in handling worldly wealth, who will trust you with _____ _____?"* (Luke 16:11).

4. If you handle His money faithfully, Christ will give you true riches— _____ ones.

5. *"Not that I am looking for a gift, but I am looking for what may be credited to your _____"* (Philippians 4:17).

6. God keeps an account open for us in heaven, and every gift given for His glory is a _____ in that account.

7. Jesus told us to give to *"the _____, the crippled, the lame, the blind…. Although they cannot repay you, you will be repaid at the _____ of the righteous"* (Luke 14:12-14).

8. If we give to those who can't _____ us, Christ guarantees He will personally reward us in heaven.

A HEART IN THE RIGHT PLACE

9. Each day brings us closer to death. If your treasures are on _____, that means each day brings you closer to _____ your treasures.

10. Jesus said, *"Where your treasure is, there your _____ will be also"* (Matthew 6:21).

Treasure Principle Key #2: My _____ always goes where I put God's money.

11. As surely as the compass needle follows north, our heart always will _____ our treasure.

12. Moses left Egypt's treasures *"because he was _____ _____ to his reward"* (Hebrews 11:26).

13. He who lays up treasures on earth spends his life backing away from his heavenly treasures. To him, death is _____. But he who lays up treasure in heaven looks forward to eternity; he's moving daily towards those treasures. To him, death is _____.

1. Look forward to your eternal rewards.
2. My heart always goes where I put God's money.

 **DISCUSSION QUESTIONS**

1. What did you hear today that was new or particularly meaningful about eternal rewards?

2. Give a personal example of your heart following your treasure.

3. What does it mean that we are constantly moving either away from or toward our treasures? How can we firmly establish that in our minds so that our decisions reflect the joy of moving toward our treasures?

EYES ON ETERNITY

4. Do you sense you are moving toward or away from your treasures? Why?

DIG DEEPER AND LEARN MORE

SCRIPTURE TO MEMORIZE
"The Son of Man is going to come in his Father's glory with his angels, and then he will reward each person according to what he has done" (Matthew 16:27).

QUESTIONS TO ANSWER

1. Read *Luke 19:12-19* and *Matthew 25:14-23*. How does our faithfulness in a small matter (worldly wealth) relate to our potential for service in eternity?

2. Read *Philippians 4:17*. What does this passage imply about an account each of us has and the way we make deposits into it?

3. Read *Luke 14:12-14* and *Matthew 6:1-5*. List at least three principles related to giving and rewards.

AUDIO TESTIMONY – JUDY

This section provides additional study and encouragement from individuals who have learned the secret of the Treasure Principle. After listening to the testimony on the CD in the back of this workbook, answer the questions below.

1. Judy talks about her family's giving to ministries going far beyond money and the impact that this holistic giving has on their hearts.

   We invest our time, our talents, and our treasures. In our giving we've had a huge privilege to see lives touched, lives changed, and the kingdom expanded. The blessings of our giving have far outweighed the gifts themselves. It's amazed us, and it's humbled us that our God could use the little bit that we give to have such an impact for the kingdom. There's no greater thrill. That verse "where your treasure is, there your heart will be also" is so true. The more we're involved with an organization, the more we give, the more we care, the more passionate we become, the more involved we become.

   Think about some of the ministries to which you give your time, talent and treasure. In what ways has your heart followed your giving in working with these ministries? Do you receive more pleasure in giving of your time or your money to these ministries? In what ways have the blessings of giving outweighed the sacrifice? Has your love for Christ grown as He enables you to give?

2. Judy also talks about the tension in giving between wanting to keep more versus following your heart and giving when God presents a need.

God showed us that is what generous giving is about. It's about going to the place where we're not comfortable and setting aside our plans and what we think we need. The thing that's come with that is great peace and joy, because we know that we're seeking God with our resources. Even though there's this tendency to pull it back in and control it myself, God's got me to the point: it is all a gift from Him, use it for Him. The biggest lesson I've learned is this: I'm not a generous giver when I give God a bigger percentage every year. I'm a generous giver when I put my hands out and say: "God, it's from you. What do you want me to do with it?"

What are the barriers that keep you from holding all of your possessions with an open hand, ready for God to use as He determines? How do you think "great peace and joy" can be experienced in being willing to go to "the place where you're not comfortable" and giving as God directs? Is the Author of your salvation also Master of your possessions?

CHAPTER 4

ROADBLOCKS TO GIVING

"Be on your guard against all kinds of greed; a man's life does not consist in the abundance of his possessions" (**Luke 12:15**).

VIDEO NOTES

Treasure Principle Key #3: _____, not earth, is my home.

1. We're _____ representing our true country.

2. *"Our citizenship is in _____"* (Philippians 3:20). We're _____ of *"a better country—a heavenly one"* (Hebrews 11:16).

3. Paradoxically, our home is a place we've never been. But it's the place we were _____ _____, the place made _____ ____.

THE MOST TOYS

4. When we die after devoting our lives to acquiring _____, we don't win—we _____.

5. Our lives have two phases: first, we have a dot. And then there's the line that extends from that dot. Our present life on earth is the dot. It begins and it ends. It's _____. But from that dot extends a line that goes _____. That line is eternity.

> Treasure Principle Key #4: I should live not for the _____ but for the line.

6. Giving is _____ _____ _____ _____ (life in heaven).

7. "He is no fool who gives what he cannot _____ to gain what he cannot _____." – Jim Elliot

POSSESSION OBSESSION

8. Material wealth doesn't make us _____.

9. We think _____ own our possessions, but too often they own _____.

THE TYRANNY OF THINGS

10. _____ _____ we buy is one more thing to think about, talk about, clean, repair, rearrange, fret over, and replace when it goes bad.

CHASING THE WIND

11. We're tempted to imagine that the earthly treasures we see around us are the genuine items rather than mere _____ of the real treasures.

12. "Any temporal possession can be turned into everlasting wealth. Whatever is given to Christ is immediately touched with _____." – A.W. Tozer

ROADBLOCKS TO GIVING

13. Giving doesn't strip me of my vested interests; rather, it shifts my vested interests from _____ to _____—from myself to God.

Mud Pies in the Slum

14. Even many Christians have settled for a life of _____ material acquisitions, like making mud pies in a slum.

Chapter Summary by Randy Alcorn

1. Heaven not earth is my home.
2. I should not live for the dot but for the line.
3. Let's not become obsessed with our possessions.
4. The more things we own, the more things actually own us.
5. Don't chase after the wind.
6. Giving is the only antidote to materialism.
7. Don't settle for a life of material acquisitions.

 DISCUSSION QUESTIONS

1. When you think of the beauty and variety of the earth, how do you envision the home in heaven that Jesus has prepared uniquely for you?

2. How did the metaphor of the junkyard affect you?

3. How do you respond to the phrase, "Live for the line, not for the dot"?

4. A.W. Tozer said, "Any temporal possession can be turned into everlasting wealth. Whatever is given to Christ is immediately touched with immortality." How does this affect your attitude toward giving possessions away? How can you transform your old way of thinking (the natural feeling of loss) into a new way of thinking (the acquired feeling of faith's positive anticipation)?

5. Recalling C.S. Lewis's metaphor of Mud Pies in the Slum, how do you respond to his statement that "we are far too easily pleased"?

DIG DEEPER AND LEARN MORE

SCRIPTURE TO MEMORIZE
"Be on your guard against all kinds of greed; a man's life does not consist in the abundance of his possessions" (Luke 12:15).

QUESTIONS TO ANSWER

1. Read *Hebrews 11:13*; *2 Corinthians 5:20*; and *Philippians 3:20*. Where is your real home? How would your life be different if that truth were a constant, conscious conviction for you?

2. Read *Hebrews 11:1*. Since our real home is a place we've never seen, why is it difficult to treat it as home, even though it was made for us and we for it?

3. Read *Hebrews 11:6* and *Romans 10:17*. What do these verses say to you about the necessity of faith and how you get it?

4. Read *1 Timothy 6:17-18*. What commands are given in these verses?

5. Now read *1 Timothy 6:19*. When Paul says, "so that they may take hold of the life that is truly life," how does it affect your perspective on everything around you? Describe a difference (other than length) between the dot and the line.

6. Read *Revelation 3:15-18*. What does this passage say to you? What contributed to their lukewarmness? How does this apply to you?

LEADING THE
WORLD
TO TRUE FINANCIAL
FREEDOM

Crown Financial Ministries™ is an interdenominational Christian organization dedicated to equipping people around the world to

LEARN · APPLY · TEACH

biblical financial principles. Since 1976, Crown has taught or equipped more than 50 million people with the life-transforming message of faithfully living by God's financial principles in every area of their lives.

Through the generosity of donors and volunteers around the globe, Crown serves followers of Christ worldwide, ranging from those entrusted with wealth to those living in desperate poverty. Regardless of their economic status, we rejoice with believers who develop a more intimate relationship with Jesus Christ, become free to serve Him, and more generously fund the Great Commission.

Help Crown build a legacy of financial free-dom for today and tomorrow. Learn more about giving and volunteer opportunities at Crown.org or call 1-800-722-1976.

CROWN FINANCIAL
MINISTRIES
True Financial Freedom

COME?LEAD?WITH?US

GLOBAL OUTREACH
On Track to Teach 300 Million by 2015

CATALYTIC EVENTS – Generous donors help Crown supply a resource package to train thousands of pastors how to teach financial freedom to their community.

PARTNERS IN MISSIONS – Crown partners alongside short-term church missions teams from across the U.S. to teach financial faithfulness.

TARGETED TEACHING TEAMS – Businesspeople volunteer to go and share their knowledge and skills with targeted leadership groups around the world.

CHURCH OUTREACH
Equipping the Church to Teach Others

FIELD STAFF – Staff and volunteers around the world help churches develop a financial ministry to raise the people and resources they need to accomplish their unique mission.

PASTOR'S CONFERENCE – Pastors and church staff are refreshed and learn how to preach, teach, celebrate, and model financial faithfulness in their churches.

LIFE GROUP STUDIES – Through Crown materials, volunteer life group leaders experience the joy of witnessing the results when people apply God's Word.

LIVE SEMINARS – Certified Volunteer Seminar Instructors teach more than 300 life-changing seminars and workshops across the U.S. every year on a variety of financial topics.

INDIVIDUAL OUTREACH
One-on-One Equipping

RADIO – Informative and engaging, our radio programs are available on over 1000 outlets around the world, online 24/7, or via Podcasting.

WEB – Our sites reach over 2 million unique visitors each year.

RESOURCES – Books, software, and audio and video resources teach True Financial Freedom.

MONEY?MAP?COACHES – Trained volunteers assist people with developing a personalized budgeting and debt reduction plan to align with their financial goals.

CHRIST@WORK – encourages and equips company owners and executive leaders and legacy leaders to impact their marketplaces for Christ by providing life groups, conferences, and biblically based resources.

Crown Money Map

The *Crown Money Map™* is the original, proven, simple step-by-step visual guide that shows you where you are and the next steps to take on your personal journey to true financial freedom. It helps you establish your life purpose, set short- and long-term goals, create an emergency savings account, and pay off consumer debt.

GOD'S ROAD MAP TO DEBT-FREE LIVING

Overwhelmed with debt? There is hope and freedom for you no matter how big your problem. Skyrocketing debt has crippled and divided millions in this age of rampant credit, interest-only mortgages, and record loan defaults. The way out from under debt burdens is not a declaration of bankruptcy, but surrender to the Word of God. Becoming debt-free may seem an impossible dream for many, but it is actually an attainable goal.

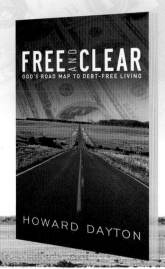

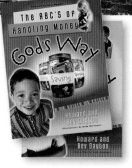

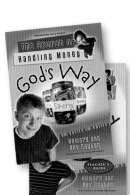

The ABC's of Handling Money God's Way

The ABC's of Handling Money God's Way uses an interesting story and fun activities to teach kids the basics about money. The 12 lessons in this book include full-color illustrations, simple Bible studies, hands-on activities, and a guided prayer journal. *Recommended for ages 5-7.*

The Secret of Handling Money God's Way

Four children with a financial challenge learn the secret of giving, saving, spending, and much more. They also discover that they can trust God to provide. This colorful, story-based workbook will engage children as they learn that God's plan for handling our finances is so much better than the world's way. *Recommended for ages 8-12.*

For more information, contact your local Christian retailer or visit us online at Crown.org

PC-BASED BUDGETING SOLUTION

The Way to Debt-Free Financial Freedom
Crown Money Map™ Financial Software

Multiplatform Compatible!
Windows®
Linux®
Mac®

The newly updated *Crown Money Map™ Financial Software* (previously *Money Matters Software™*) is designed to ease your financial burdens by doing a lot of the thinking for you. This software will lead you through the process of examining all your income and expenses, and the unique feature is that the software will teach you how to create a reasonable spending and savings plan.

This newly revised software for 2006/2007 will provide you with all you need to become financially free.

FREE 30-day trial available.

WEB-BASED BUDGETING SOLUTION

CROWN™
Mvelopes **Personal** ®
Web-Based Budgeting Tool

FREE 30 DAY TRIAL

Why is it so difficult to manage our spending?

It's mainly because we have lost the tie with physical cash. Today we live in a near cashless society–using debit cards, credit cards, automatic deposits, online bill payments, and so on. We rarely even see our money. It's easier than ever to spend, spend, spend! And tracking your spending is virtually impossible. That's where **Crown™ Mvelopes® Personal** comes in!

The solution is simple!

Crown Mvelopes Personal is a spending management system that modernizes the traditional Envelope Budeting Method, using advanced computer technology and the Internet.

Get started with a FREE 30-day Trial of Crown Mvelopes Personal today!

To sign up and to get your free 30-day trial, visit
Crown.Mvelopes.com.

CASH AND BILL ORGANIZERS

The Cash Organizer™ envelope budgeting system will simplify your budgeting plan by keeping you in control of your cash spending. If there's no money left in a particular budget envelope, you're finished spending in that category until payday! English/Spanish Bilingual Edition

With the *Bill Organizer™*, there's no more searching frantically for that misplaced phone bill or wondering if the power bill has been paid! This expanding file can be customized easily to organize your bills by either category or due date! Bonus audio CD message included.

For more information, contact your local Christian retailer or visit us online at Crown.org

AUDIO TESTIMONY – BRUCE AND SUE

This section provides additional study and encouragement from individuals who have learned the secret of the Treasure Principle. After listening to the testimony on the CD in the back of this workbook, answer the questions below.

1. Sue talks about the two Russian girls who lived with the family for a few weeks. When she took the girls back to the airport to fly home, she asked them whether they would miss America. The girls' reply shocked her.

   One of the girls said, "I never want to be like you Americans. You spend all your time taking care of your things. Your husband works to buy a house that takes all of your time to take care of. You buy new clothes. You wash them and iron them and take them to the dry cleaners. You have two cars that you have to service and you wash and vacuum them." I felt ashamed to be an American. I felt ashamed at what my life represented at that point. Even though I loved the Lord and we were doing some great things, I saw how someone else viewed my life. That was a wakeup call for us.

   How has your time been reallocated as your income has risen and you've accumulated more things? How has this impacted your relationship with God either positively or negatively? In light of this, do you see what Jesus meant when he said you can't serve both God and Money? Explain.

2. As this couple has progressed on their journey of generosity, their view on how God views their possessions and giving has changed as expressed in the following statement by Bruce.

God is not only interested in our income; He was also interested in our assets. It wasn't just a question of what percent of our income we were going to give away, He wanted our balance sheet as well. One of the things Henry Blackaby said at a past Generous Giving conference was when God returns, is He going to be pleased in the amount you've accumulated versus the amount you've given away? Is He going to be pleased in the amount you've invested in this world versus the amount you've invested in eternity?

Are there any assets that you consider "hands off" regarding your giving to God? If so, list them. What steps can you take to help free your heart from the hold of these possessions? When Christ returns, will he be pleased at the amount you've invested in the world versus the amount you've invested in eternity? Why or why not?

CHAPTER 5

GETTING STARTED

*"I have held many things in my hands
and I have lost them all. But whatever I have placed in God's hands,
that I still possess."*
—Martin Luther

 **VIDEO NOTES**

1. *"A tithe of everything from the land, whether grain from the soil or fruit from
   the trees, belongs to the Lord; it is _____ to the Lord"* (Leviticus 27:30).
   The meaning of the word "tithe" is a _____ part.

2. Proverbs 3:9 says, *"Honor the Lord with your wealth, with the firstfruits of
   all your crops."* God's children give to Him _____, not _____.

TRAINING WHEELS

3. But it seems fair to ask, "God, do you really _____ _____ of me than
   You demanded of the poorest Israelite when I have Your Holy Spirit living
   within me and I live in the wealthiest society in human history?"

4. God doesn't expect us all to give the _____ amount. God tells us in
   Deuteronomy that we're to give in _____ to how He's
   blessed us.

5. Ironically, many people cannot afford to give because they're _____ _____. (Haggai 1:9-11).

6. It's much easier to live on 90 percent or 50 percent or 10 percent of your income _____ the will of God than it is to live on 100 percent _____ it.

Excellent Giving

7. *"See that you also excel in this grace of giving"* (2 Corinthians 8:7). Like piano playing, giving is a _____. With _____, we get better at it.

Give It Now or Give It Later?

8. Zaccheus said, *"Here and now I give half of my possessions . . ."* (Luke 19:8). If you procrastinate, the same heart that's prompting you to give today may later persuade you not to. Why? Because as a result of _____ giving, your heart's vested interests _____ on earth and _____ in heaven.

9. Death isn't your _____ opportunity to give; it's the _____ of your opportunity to give.

What Will We Leave the Kids?

10. Leaving a large inheritance to children is not just a _____ opportunity to invest in God's kingdom. It's also rarely in the _____ best interests.

11. Your children should love the Lord, work hard, and experience the joy of _____ God.

12. Jesus said, *"Give, and it will be _____ to you. A good measure, pressed down, shaken together and running over, will be poured into your lap. For with the measure you use, it will be measured to you"* (Luke 6:38). The more you give, the more comes back to you, because God is the greatest giver in the universe, and He won't let you _____ Him.

13. Paul tells us exactly why He provides us with more money than we need: *"Now he who supplies seed to the sower and bread for food will also supply and _____ your store of seed…"* (2 Corinthians 9:10). *"You will be made rich in every way so that you can be _____ on every occasion"* (2 Corinthians 9:11).

> Treasure Principle Key #6: God prospers me not to raise my standard of _____, but to raise my standard of _____.

14. *"At the present time your _____ will supply what they need, so that in turn their plenty will supply what you _____. Then there will be equality, as it is written: 'He who gathered much did not have too much, and he who gathered little did not have too little'"* (2 Corinthians 8:14-15). Why does God give some of His children _____ than they need and others less than they need? So that He may use His children to _____ _____ _____.

CHAPTER SUMMARY

1. Begin by giving a tithe.
2. The tithe is God's historical method to get us on the path of giving.
3. Giving is a skill that needs practice.
4. Learn to give as much as you can.
5. Let God decide how much to provide for your adult children.
6. The more you give, the more comes back to you.
7. God prospers me not to raise my standard of living but to raise my standard of giving.

GETTING STARTED

 **DISCUSSION QUESTIONS**

1. Do you think training wheels is a good analogy for tithing? Why or why not?

2. How do you respond to the idea that many people can't afford to give generously—precisely because they're not giving?

3. Remember Scott, the guy who laughed when Bill Bright challenged some people to give a million dollars but then grew in his giving as God blessed him? Don't worry about the numbers for a moment; just consider the concept. Discuss the principle and its application for anyone at any income level.

4. In what ways could you begin implementing the principle of giving more now rather than trying to amass a large amount to give later or when you die?

5. What do you think about the principle that God gives some of His children more than they need and others less than they need so that He may use them to help one another?

DIG DEEPER AND LEARN MORE

SCRIPTURE TO MEMORIZE
"See that you also excel in this grace of giving"
(2 Corinthians 8:7).

QUESTIONS TO ANSWER

1. Read *Malachi 3:8-10*. Do you think God is serious about our giving? Why do you think it's so important to Him?

2. Read *Haggai 1:9-11*. Do you really believe that God can orchestrate events in such a way that they appear to be merely natural? Can you think of events in your own past that might have turned out quite differently if you had been faithfully acting as God's manager rather than a self-absorbed owner?

3. Read *2 Corinthians 9:10-14*. In verse 11, Paul says that *"you will be made rich in every way."* What reason does He give for God doing this?

4. Verses 13 and 14 mention several benefits for the gift the Corinthians have promised. List them.

5. Read *2 Corinthians 8:13-15*. How does the basic principle of this passage conflict with the competitive mindset our culture has—thinking that people prove their worth by outperforming and out-earning others?

AUDIO TESTIMONY – SCOTT

This section provides additional study and encouragement from individuals who have learned the secret of the Treasure Principle. After listening to the testimony on the CD in the back of this workbook, answer the questions below.

1. Scott has a unique view of the reason God kept him in business instead of sending him to a foreign country as a missionary, as seen in his following statement:

   I am a missionary. I am using the skills and talents that God gave me to do business for the purpose of making money to fund the fulfillment of the Great Commission. It is the most liberating experience to truly have God running your business, because when the big deal falls apart—big deal. It is His deal when it comes through, praise the Lord, and then we get to go shopping (for kingdom opportunities).

   If you own a business or work for an employer, why has God blessed you with the skills and opportunities to make money? In what ways can you experience liberation from greed, unhealthy competition and other sinful desires by letting God run your business/career?

2. There are a couple of eye-opening statistics that Scott shares in his testimony regarding the current allocation of Christian giving to domestic versus overseas mission work:

I had never heard before that 80 percent of the Christian wealth of the world was in America and that 96 percent of what we put in the plate was spent on America and that America only made up roughly 5 or 6 percent of the world's population. And I immediately was troubled when I heard that, knowing that the Scripture said, "To whom much has been given, much is required."

How do you currently divide your giving between national and international ministry work? What are some adjustments that you might need to make in view of this?

CHAPTER 6

FOR SUCH A TIME AS THIS

> *"It ought to be the business of every day to prepare for our last day."*
> —Matthew Henry

 ## VIDEO NOTES

FIVE MINUTES AFTER WE DIE

1. Christians don't receive a second chance to live life over—doing more to help the needy and invest in God's kingdom. We have _____ _____ opportunity—a lifetime on earth—to use our resources to make a difference.

2. Ask yourself, *Five minutes after I die, what will I _____ I would have given away while I still had the chance?*

Write your own obituary. Please turn to the "Dig Deeper and Learn More" section on page 48, when instructed by the workshop video, and use questions 1 and 2 for this exercise.

THE GIFT OF GIVING

3. Scripture tells us not to give *in order to* be seen by men (Matthew 6:1). Certainly we should be careful to avoid pride. But Jesus also said, *Let your light shine before men, that they may _____ your good deeds and praise your Father in heaven"* (Matthew 5:16).

4. Through an unfortunate misinterpretation of biblical teaching, we've _____ giving under a basket. As a result, we're not teaching Christians to give. And they're lacking joy and _____ because of it.

5. King David told the people exactly how much he'd given to build the temple. The precise amounts of gold and precious stones given by the leaders were also made public. *"The people rejoiced at the willing response of their _____, for they had given freely and wholeheartedly to the Lord"* (1 Chronicles 29:6-9).

A Sense of Destiny

6. Remember what Mordecai said to Esther? *"If you remain silent at this time, relief and deliverance for the Jews will arise from _____ place, but you and your father's family will perish. And who knows but that you have come to royal position for _____ __ _____ as this?"* (Esther 4:14).

7. Remind yourself again why the God of providence has _____ you with so much: *"Your plenty will supply what they need...so that you can be _____ on every occasion"* (2 Corinthians 8:14; 9:11).

8. Why not set a figure you can _____ ____, then tell God that everything He provides beyond that amount you'll give back to Him?

9. Let's give until our hearts are more in touch with God's _____ _____ than with our remodeling projects, business ventures, dream vacations, or retirement plans.

Thoughts to Consider

10. Giving should start with your local Bible-believing, Christ-centered _____, the spiritual community to which you are accountable. Beyond that, you can generously support worthy missions and parachurch _____, carefully evaluating them by biblical standards.

My Giving Covenant

1. I affirm God's full ownership of me and everything entrusted to me.

2. I set aside the firstfruits—at least 10 percent—of every wage and gift I receive as holy and belonging exclusively to the Lord.

3. Out of the remaining treasures God entrusts to me, I seek to make generous freewill gifts.

4. I ask God to teach me to give sacrificially to His purposes, including helping the poor and reaching the lost.

5. Recognizing that I cannot take earthly treasures from this world, I determine to lay them up as heavenly treasures—for Christ's glory and the eternal good of others and myself.

6. I ask God to show me how to lead others to the present joy and future reward of the Treasure Principle.

Signed: _____

Witness: _____

Date:_____

11. *"The Lord Jesus himself said: 'It is _____ _____ to give than to receive'"* (Acts 20:35).

12. "We're so absorbed with "getting what's _____" that we miss what brings the real blessing and joy—giving God what's _____.

13. "Embrace Christ's invitation: *"Give, and it will be _____ to you"* (Luke 6:38). Then when He gives you more, remind yourself why: that you may be generous on every occasion.

CHAPTER SUMMARY BY RANDY ALCORN

1. Five minutes after we die, we'll know exactly how we should have lived.
2. Giving is for everyone.
3. Develop a sense of destiny.
4. When you give, you'll feel His pleasure.

DISCUSSION QUESTIONS

1. Recalling Alfred Nobel's story, how do you think your friends would summarize your life? What would they see as your greatest contribution to the world so far? What do you think would stand out to them as having been most important to you?

2. What do you think God would say was most important to you?

3. What would you like God and others to say was most important to you? Are you moving in that direction?

4. Imagine your thoughts five minutes after you die. Try to describe what you imagine.

5. How does the perspective that you are among the world's wealthy strike you?

6. Have you set a figure you can live on, telling God that everything He provides beyond that amount (adjusted for inflation) will be given back to Him? If not, will you pray about it now and consider setting a figure within the next 30 days?

7. Have you signed the Giving Covenant? If not, will you pray about it and consider signing it now?

8 What have you purposed to do with this covenant?

 ## DIG DEEPER AND LEARN MORE

 ### SCRIPTURE TO MEMORIZE
"Let your light shine before men, that they may see your good deeds and praise your Father in heaven" (Matthew 5:16).

QUESTIONS TO ANSWER

1. Take a few minutes to do the valuable exercise mentioned after Alfred Nobel's story: Think about what your obituary would say if it were written today. What would others say characterized your life? Write them down.

2. Now write your obituary from heaven's perspective. Think in terms of deeds, not merely good intentions. What would God find notable about your life?

My "Heavenly" Obituary

3. As you look at your answers to the two preceding questions, what changes would you like to make in your values and lifestyle to improve those answers?

4. Read *Matthew 7:9-12* and *22:36-40*. Is it possible to love without giving? How does God connect the two? Since "all the law and the prophets hang on these two commandments," how important do you think they are to God? How much do you think they will count toward your final grade?

Note: If you desire to participate in additional studies to learn what the Lord says about how to handle money, including spending, saving, investing, giving, getting out of debt, and much more, please contact Crown Financial Ministries at www.Crown.org or call 800-722-1976.

PRAYER REQUESTS

*"Pray for each other. . . . The
prayer of a righteous man is
powerful and effective"*
(James 5:16).

B EFORE YOU END EACH SESSION, YOU MAY WANT TO TAKE
prayer requests. There is one page for each chapter for you to
record these requests. Please consider praying daily for those
in your workshop group.

CHAPTER 1 PRAYER LOG

Date	Prayer Request(s)	Answers to Prayer

CHAPTER 2 PRAYER LOG

Date	Prayer Request(s)	Answers to Prayer

CHAPTER 3 PRAYER LOG

Date	Prayer Request(s)	Answers to Prayer

CHAPTER 4 PRAYER LOG

Date	Prayer Request(s)	Answers to Prayer

CHAPTER 5 PRAYER LOG

Date	Prayer Request(s)	Answers to Prayer

CHAPTER 6 PRAYER LOG

Date	Prayer Request(s)	Answers to Prayer

ANSWER KEY

CHAPTER 1
1. treasure, joy
2. 15
3. treasure, money
4. inseparable
5. money
6. reward
7. heavenly
8. worthless
9. heart
10. last
11. always
12. investment, treasures
13. commands
14. take, send
15. eternity
16. temporal
17. million

Discussion Questions
Personal answers

Dig Deeper and Learn More Questions
1. 1. The length of our earthly future is uncertain. 2. God does not want us to hoard, thinking only of ourselves. 3. Everything we hoard will end up going to someone else.
2. We are to be rich toward God. The second is a personal answer, but this is an example: I should recognize Him as the source of my security and joy. I should use the resources He blesses me with to meet the needs of others as well as my own.
3. Personal answer

CHAPTER 2
1. belongs
2. everything
   Treasure Principle Key #1: everything
3. steward
4. managers, Owner's
5. account
6. live on
7. giving, cheerful
8. after
9. poverty, generosity
10. luxury, poor
11. pleaded
12. grace
13. grace
14. joy
15. Lord
16. worship
17. poor, not
18. freedom
19. Giving, eternal

Discussion Questions
1. We can more easily see material possessions as secondary to our real life and purpose.

Loss through circumstances beyond our control need not threaten us. He has no shortage of resources. He can entrust to us whatever He chooses whenever He knows it is best.
2. The best places to invest the Owner's money are those that Scripture describes. We invest in opportunities to evangelize, disciple, help and feed the needy. We help those who cannot repay.
3. He gave first. He set the example and He provides both the desire and the means. The same Greek word is used for Christian giving as for God's grace.
4. Giving is an act of worship when we give ourselves to God first. Everything we give for the benefit of others is accepted by Christ as a gift to Him. Our giving is primarily to God, and only secondarily to the pastor or the church.
5. Giving brings us closer to God, making us more open to what He has for us. Giving causes us to feel God's pleasure. Giving is one way we worship God. Giving empowers our prayer life. Giving frees us from the pressure of possessions. Giving infuses life with joy. Giving interjects an eternal dimension into ordinary life.
6. Personal answer

Dig Deeper and Learn More Questions
1. The Lord owns everything. Personal answer to second question.
2. 1. Whoever can be trusted with little can be trusted with much. 2. Whoever is dishonest with little will be dishonest with much. 3. If you are not trustworthy with worldly wealth, you will not be trusted with the true riches (for example, intimacy with Christ). 4. If you are not a trustworthy manager, you will not be given more to manage. 5. You cannot serve both God and money. 6. Those who have been given a trust must prove faithful.
3. 1. They gave out of the grace God had given them. 2. They gave even though they were

in a severe trial themselves. 3. They gave in spite of extreme poverty. 4. Their overflowing joy resulted in rich generosity. 5. They gave beyond their ability. 6. They urgently pleaded for the privilege of giving. 7. They gave to serve the saints. 8. They gave themselves to the Lord first. 9. They obeyed God's leading in their giving.
4. He is very concerned with their needs. Jesus says that when we have met the needs of others, we have ministered to him. His plan for the needy employs the principle of sowing and reaping for us. When we give, everyone benefits, but we benefit most of all because of joy now and eternal rewards later.

Audio Testimony
Personal answers

CHAPTER 3
1. heaven
2. reward
3. true riches
4. eternal
5. account
6. deposit
7. poor, resurrection
8. reward
9. earth, losing
10. heart
    Treasure Principle Key #2: heart
11. follow
12. looking ahead
13. loss, gain

Discussion Questions
Personal answers

Dig Deeper and Learn More Questions
1. If we are faithful with what is entrusted to our management in this life, God will increase our potential for service in eternity. Service to the King, like giving, results in great joy—sharing the Master's happiness.
2. God keeps a heavenly account for each of us and credits to it the deposits we make by giving here on earth. This is an example of giving "what we cannot keep to gain that which we cannot lose" as said by Jim Elliot.
3. 1. Give to those who cannot repay you so that you will be repaid at the resurrection. 2.

God lets no good deed go unrewarded. 3. If you give in order to be honored by men, you have your reward already. 4. When you give in secret, God will reward you. (Whose reward would you rather have?)

Audio Testimony
   Personal answers

CHAPTER 4
   Treasure Principle Key #3: Heaven
1.   ambassadors
2.   heaven, citizens
3.   made for, for us
4.   things, lose
5.   brief, forever
   Treasure Principle Key #4: dot
6.   living for the line
7.   keep, lose
8.   happy
9.   we, us
10.   Every item
11.   shadows
12.   immortality
   Treasure Principle Key #5: antidote
13.   earth, heaven
14.   unsatisfying

Discussion Questions
1-3. Personal answers
4.   Personal answer. In response to the second part: Meditating on the Scriptures that reveal the contrast between earth and heaven will renew your mind and transform your worldview (Romans 12:2).
5.   Personal answer

Dig Deeper and Learn More Questions
1.   Our real home is heaven. The second part is personal.
2.   Faith is required for us to accept something we've never seen as being more real than what we see around us every day.
3.   We can't please God without it. We must believe not only that He exists but also that He rewards those who earnestly seek Him. Our faith comes from God's Word. It takes increased exposure to His Word to increase our faith.
4.   1. Do not be arrogant. 2. Do not put your hope in wealth, which is so uncertain. 3. Put your hope in God, who richly provides everything for your enjoyment. 4. Be rich in good deeds. 5. Be generous. 6. Be willing to share.

5.   Personal answer. In response to the second part: The reality we see around us every day (the dot) is not life as God intended. Only when we are with Him will we experience the real thing. In the meantime, we can prepare for it and experience the enjoyment of God's provision in its proper perspective.
6.   When we think we are wealthy and don't need anything from God, in reality, we are "wretched, pitiful, poor, blind and naked." Our warped perception (Satan's deception) blinds us to reality. Unless we see the truth and change direction, we risk God's judgment.

Audio Testimony
   Personal answers

CHAPTER 5
1.   holy, tenth
2.   first, last
3.   expect less
4.   same, proportion
5.   not giving
6.   inside, outside
7.   skill, practice
8.   postponing, increase, decrease
9.   best, end
10.   missed, children's
11.   trusting
12.   given, outgive
13.   increase, generous
   Treasure Principle Key #6: living, giving
14.   plenty, need, more, help one another

Discussion Questions
   Personal answers

Dig Deeper and Learn More Questions
1.   Yes. The second part is a personal answer. Consider: 1. He doesn't need what we give, but He knows that we need to give in recognition of our dependence on Him. 2. When we give to Him, our hearts follow. 3. When we give to Him, we fulfill His plan for us to meet each other's needs and demonstrate love that the world doesn't understand. 4. When we give to Him, we store up treasures in heaven to be enjoyed forever; as a loving Father, He wants the best for us.
2.   Personal answers
3.   "So that you can be generous on every occasion."
4.   1. It will supply the needs of

God's people. 2. It results in many people giving expressions of thanks to God. 3. It allows them the opportunity to prove themselves. 4. Men will praise God for the obedience that accompanies their confession of the gospel of Christ (their credibility is enhanced by their willingness to put their money where their mouth is). 5. Men will praise God for their generosity in sharing with them and everyone else. 6. Others will pray for the Corinthians in a heartfelt way.
5.   Twice in this passage, Paul uses the word equality. It's all about sharing so that everyone's needs can be met. Paul quotes the Exodus 16:18 passage that describes God's provision of manna (bread) for His people. Read the Exodus story and notice that God specifically instructed the people to gather only what they could eat that day. He did not want them to hoard. This story contains several principles for us. Put yourself in God's place: As a loving parent, would you prefer your children to compete in a way that they starve each other out? Or would you prefer them to be generous with each other and work to establish a reasonable level of equality even though their gifts, abilities and opportunities vary?

Audio Testimony
   Personal answers

CHAPTER 6
1.   one brief
2.   wish
3.   see
4.   hidden, purpose
5.   leaders
6.   another, such a time
7.   entrusted, generous
8.   live on
9.   kingdom work
10.   church, ministries
11.   more blessed
12.   ours, His
13.   given

Discussion Questions
   Personal answers

Dig Deeper and Learn More Questions
   Personal answers

For additional reading, purchase the book that is the foundation for *The Treasure Principle Workshop*!

Best-selling author Randy Alcorn introduces readers to a revolution in material freedom and radical generosity that will change lives around the world. Ninety-five percent of Christians have never come to terms with a biblical perspective on their material possessions, Alcorn writes.

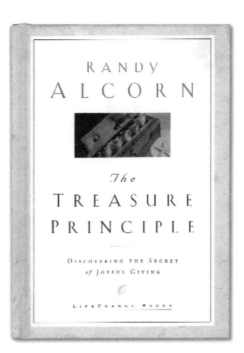

God has entrusted His wealth to us and called upon us to manage and invest His money. This is in everyone's best interest, including our own. When Jesus told His followers to "lay up for yourselves treasures in heaven," He intended that they discover an astounding secret: how joyful giving brings God maximum glory and His children maximum pleasure.

The Treasure Principle
ISBN 1-57673-780-2
94 pages, hardcover

Available at your local Christian retailer and www.GenerousGiving.org.

INVOLVEMENT AND SUGGESTIONS

We want to hear from you!

- Did you enjoy this workshop?
- What kind of impact did it have on your personal finances?
- Did your financial outlook improve during the workshop?
- Did this study meet your expectations?
- Do you have any suggestions for improving the workshop?

After you have completed this workshop, would you take a few minutes and share your personal comments, suggestions, and stories with us? We sincerely value your input as we strive to make our resources better.

Log in to Crown.org/Workshops and look for the "Involvement and Suggestions" link. Your comments are confidential and will only be used to improve this workshop.

Thank you in advance for your willingness to share your experience in this workshop with us!